Table of Contents

All sections within this book contain high-frequency words.

Quick review of book 1 *Learn to Read Early*, (Early Readers Volume 1)....................3-9
Simple plural endings in words with rules covered thus far..10-11
'ck' endings in words with short vowels..12
'Y' ending words..13-15
'wh' words...16
'oy' 'oi' words...17
Long list of words in categories by pattern..18-26
Contractions, rule in words with rules covered thus far..27
An introduction to compound words..28
'l' controlled vowel 'a'...29
'r' controlled vowels..30-32
'aw' 'ew' and 'ow' words...33-36
'le' endings..37
Vowel + Consonant + 'e' rule..38-40
'c' sounds like 'k' and 'c' sounds like 's' rule..41-42
High-frequency word list (intermixed rules covered thus far)...43-56
'er' endings 57
'a' beginnings...58
Some 2 and 3 syllable high-frequency word covered in rules thus far........................58-59
Introduction to 'ed' endings..59
The **key** to learning to read..60
Reference chart...61-62

This section contains a brief review of the previous book *Learn to Read Early*. Please review these words as a refresher.

Short vowel sound for 'a'

| sat | hat | mat |
| ran | fan | man |

Short vowel sound for 'e'

| pet | jet | let |
| set | hen | pen |

Short vowel sound for 'i'

| pin | fin | win |
| fit | pit | mit |

Short vowel sound for 'o'

| hot | got | pot |
| fog | log | hog |

Welcome back to those who have discovered this book series. Your child/student has had the opportunity of having all these letter patterns with explanations in one place in a language (s)he can understand rather than fragments of information on occasion, and the memorization of new words at random. Your student/child is organizing words based on logic. This influences abilities in reading, spelling, writing, logical thinking, and general patterns.

The words build on a progression based on intricate factors. The amount of words per list that a child can handle were very important to the first book. This book assumes the child has some reading momentum and understands the rules presented in the first book. Certain words with individual letters that are known to cause confusion with children were used in moderation, and introduced slowly to allow the new reader to gain momentum. Vowel and consonant combinations as well. And words such as 'hard', 'fear', 'can't were avoided as they're demotivating.

Reading by understanding is for the young beginning reader as well as an established reader who simply needs to add understanding. Passivity in decoding is thereby voided and confidence can rule. Understanding words in this way will change a person's life!

This book is meant to be studied in order and reviewed regularly. Reviewing previous word groups is encouraged, but many times skipping ahead is not advised.

The more this book is reviewed, the stronger the neuronal pathways, the larger the connections, and the bigger the imprint of the reader's reference base.

Throughout this book you will be presented with many words. The teacher should provide assistance reading full words as needed and help "sound out" or "think out" words by offering letter sounds, not letter names. You are encouraged to ask the student to "try again" at times before offering help, especially once the teacher is aware the student is familiar with the sound and "knows it". The teacher and student should always place an index finger under the letter for which the letter sound is being made. Always use your finger to point under the words you read to your child, without exception (in all books you read), and teach your student/child to do the same.

Check out books from your local library and make it exciting when you recognize words from this book in your library books and from one book in another book. Make it exciting to find similar words with similar sounds and words that follow the same rules.

Find out how many books you can check-out at your local library. Different libraries have different maximums allowed. Some libraries allow an unlimited amount. I have checked-out an average of 75 books every few weeks from my local public library and all for free (both fiction and nonfiction). You can renew your books and when your student becomes attached, you can explain "we can check them out again." The more books your student is exposed to the quicker (s)he will be reading. And combined with learning to read by understanding the letter patterns in words you will assure that your student has the best chance at becoming a successful reader.

You are encouraged to use positive reinforcement and compliments. Use phrases such as "good job," "wow," "excellent," "that's amazing," "you did it," "you are such a good reader," "you try and try again," "you're so smart," etc. You may also choose to offer fun activities as a response to the student's efforts such as, trips to the zoo, trips to the library, trips to the park, etc. Tell others about your student's amazing efforts and abilities while your student is listening. Make reading a part of your routine and a large part of your life.

You will encounter words in reading materials that do not "follow the rules". These rule breakers are in the minority, and the majority follow the rules. Some of the rule breakers are high frequency words, also known as sight words, which means they are the same words which reappear again and again. The portion of high frequency words that do break the rules will need to be memorized at a point when reading by understanding is established and the student can understand that there are some rule breakers that need to be memorized. Exposure to books and reading will accelerate their recognition for less labored memorization.

It is important to practice reading the words in this book regularly. Some may do it weekly. Some make practice daily. Make this book and reading books a part of your routine. Encourage your student to read SLOWLY and to read one word before moving his/her eyes and finger to the next word(s).

Short vowel sound for 'u'

hut   fun   hun
run   sun

When two e's are next to each other they say long 'e'. Let the teacher pretend to be an 'e' and the student pretend to be the other 'e' and say long 'e' at the same time for fun. Then review these words.

meet   feet   see
green   sleep   tree

When the 't' and 'h' are next to each other like this, they make a 'th' sound. They are silly, when they get together, they say their regular sounds when they're not together, but together they make a new sound. Make it funny.

this   that   then
bath   math   with

There are two main sounds the 'oo' make, review them in the following words.

spoon　　　boot　　　food
book　　　foot　　　took

There are words that end in 'ing'.

sleeping　　　looking　　　seeing
mixing　　　fixing　　　jumping

Vowels

a e i o u and sometimes y

Consonants

b c d f g h j k l m n p q

r s t v w x y z

The 'ai' pattern is most commonly the long 'a' pattern. When these two letters get together in this order, it reads as the long 'a' sound and the 'i' is silent. "When [these] two vowels are walking the first one does the talking". Compare this situation to two people who get together and one talks while the other doesn't. Move the book around the room as though it is walking.

hair	wait	paint
snail	rain	train

When 'ea' get together in this order, the 'e' sound is read and the 'a' is silent. It's most often the long 'e' pattern, but sometimes a short 'e' pattern. There are exceptions as in "bear," "heart," and "wear." "When [these] two vowels are walking the first one does the talking". Compare this situation to two people who get together and one talks while the other doesn't. Move the book around the room as though it is walking.

neat	hear	ear
cream	dear	clean

There is a long vowel letter pattern 'oa'. When these two letters get together in this order, the 'o' sound is read and the 'a' is silent. It's most commonly a long 'o' pattern. "When [these] two vowels are walking the first one does the talking". Compare this situation to two people who get together and one talks while the other doesn't. Move the book around the room as though it is walking.

boat	goat	coat
soap	road	throat

There is a long vowel letter pattern 'ue'. When these two letters get together in this order, the long 'u' sound is read and the 'e' is silent. "When [these] two vowels are walking the first one does the talking". Compare this situation to two people who get together and one talks while the other doesn't. Move the book around the room as though it is walking.

blue	true	glue
clue		

Some short words have two consonants next to each other. These words can be read as though they are one sound and that's okay! Double consonants in short words are seen with these letters 'nn' 'dd' 'tt' 'ss' 'ff' 'll' and 'zz'.

pass	mess	sell
bell	hill	kiss

The 'y' is sometimes a vowel. This happens when the 'y' is at the end, or in the middle of a word (at the beginning of words 'y' is a consonant). There is an 'ay' pattern that is found at the ends words. The 'a' is long and the 'y' is considered silent. It also follows the rule: "When [these] two vowels are walking, the first one does the talking." However, if one chooses to say the sound of consonant 'y' in this 'ay' pattern that is fine!

may	play	way
stay	say	day

The 'ou' sound produced in most words is as in these words.

out	loud	shout
proud	ouch	count

When 'igh' are next to each other they make the long 'i' sound and the gh are silent.

night	light	bright
right	sigh	high

Some words end in 'er' and it sounds like this:

sticker   marker   letter
after   helper   liver

When 'sh' letters are next to each other like this they make a new sound. They are silly when they get together they make a new sound.

sheep   shop   shut
brush   shout   fish

When 'ch' letters are next to each other like this they make a new sound. They are silly when they get together they make a new sound. Most often the sound is 'ch' as in "chair", it can also sound like 'k' in less than about 100 common words. It can also sound like 'sh', rarely and be silent very rarely.

chair   chip   chin
cheek   lunch   inch

This point marks the end of our review. Here we introduce plural endings. Give an example, 'there can be 1 frog and there can be 2 or more frogs... I can have 1 cup or I can have 2 cups, or more cups, 3 cups, 4 cups!' Emphasize the 's' sound when you provide examples. Practice and return frequently. For words ending in s, x, z, ch or sh, add -es.

hats	nets	years
boots	pounds	hens
spoons	flags	pots
eggs	fans	trees
troops	hooks	cloths

Plural endings with 'es' in 's' 'x' 'z' 'ch' and 'sh'

busses   dresses   glasses

boxes   foxes   buzzes

lunches   dishes

Some words end in 'ck' and it just sounds like 'k'. Oh how wonderful! 'ck' can also be found in the middle of words too, but not at the beginnings. Practice and return frequently.

duck	kick	neck
lock	clock	brick
rock	truck	sock
back	pack	stack
trick	lick	

When 'y' is the first letter in words, it is a consonant, like in 'yes' and 'yellow'. The letter 'y' is considered a vowel when it's anywhere other than the first letter. It is considered a vowel because it can sound like 'e' 'i' or be silent. We have seen 'ay' words where the 'a' is long and the 'y' is considered silent, some pronounce it as a 'y' sounding consonant and that's fine. Let's review.

play	say	day
way	tray	stay
may	spray	away

Practice the 'ey' words, the 'e' in this pattern is long. It's fine to think of the 'y' here sounding like a consonant 'y' or a silent 'y'. You may use the two vowels walking rule just like with the 'ay' or pronounce the 'y' if you prefer. Practice and return frequently.

key	monkey	donkey
honey	valley	chimney

Practice the 'y' sounding like an 'e' in adjectives and some other words. Notice here the 'y' is following a consonant and sounds like an 'e'. Practice and return frequently.

funny	happy	rainy
happy	carry	silly
bunny	mommy	daddy
sandy	sticky	sunny
many	easy	very
body	any	study

Practice the 'y' sounding like an 'i' following a consonant. This doesn't happen with many words. Practice and return frequently.

my   try   fry

shy   by   sky

When the 'wh' letters are next to each other like this we usually say the 'w' sound and the 'h' is silent. Practice and return frequently.

what   when   why

which   wheel   whip

whisper

Practice the 'oy' words. 'oy' makes the sound found in the following words. Practice and return frequently.

boy   toy   joy

soy   ploy

When the 'oi' letters are next to each other as such, they produce the following sound. Practice and return frequently.

coin   soil   oink

foil   point   spoil

join   moist   toilet

toil   oil

The following are high-frequency words separated into groups by letter patterns. Practice and return frequently.

'ea' words:

each	year	years
seat	read	eat
near	hear	weak
real	clear	heat
deal	speak	lead
least	beat	ears

stream meat east

clean team reach

reached

'Oa words'

road boat coast

'th' words

that	with	cloths
this	then	then
them	than	thing
things	think	three

'ee' words

deep	sleep	free
trees	see	need
keep	tree	seem
feet	steel	seen
feel	street	
week		
meet	speed	

'ou' words

pound	out	sound
our	found	south
ground	round	noun
pounds	count	cloud
mouth	loud	around
about		

'oo'

boots	spoons	troops
tools	too	food
soon	room	moon
root	poor	cool
hooks	books	look
good	took	book

stood   cook   wood

'ay' words

way			day			may

play		stay		lay

pay			away

'ai' words

air			wait		pair

paint		rain		train

main		hair		sail

fair

'igh' words

right   hight   light

might   night   bright

fight   sight

It is helpful to teach contractions, and it's great to practice reading them without being unsure of that little line up there. What is that? The apostrophe that signifies a contraction. The apostrophe specifically takes the place of the ONE LETTER (THE VOWEL) that is missing from the second word. For example, look carefully at the phrase 'do not' the contraction is: 'don't and the apostrophe takes the place of the 'o' in 'not'. This happens the same way in each contraction. Explain what is happening with contractions, but it's fine to practice reading contractions even if the logic behind the contraction isn't fully learned yet. The more exposure and practice the sooner it will be mastered. The following contractions contain rules we've gone over.

did not..........................didn't
I will................................ I'll
has not.......................... hasn't
it is.................................. it's
let us.............................. let's
is not.............................. isn't

didn't   I'll   hasn't
it's   let's   isn't

This is a brief introduction to compound words, to know they exist, they can be exciting! Compound words happen when two words are stuck together to make one word.

however	himself
herself	without
toothbrush	hotdog
mailbox	within

When the 'a' is followed by the 'l' and looks as though it should sounds like a short 'a' and doesn't it is because it is followed by an 'l'. This is an l-controlled 'a'. The 'a' sounds like that because of the 'l' that comes right after it.

all	small	ball
fall	tall	mall
salt	chalk	call
hall	wall	

Some words appear to follow the letter patterns where a short vowel sound seem like it should be produced, however it sounds different because there is a letter 'r' following the vowel. These are called r-controlled vowels. The 'r' makes the vowel just before it sound a little funny.

'ar'

mark	far	car
farm	park	star
start	arm	barn
yard	art	dollars
chart		

'er'

verb   never   tower

ruler   marker   sister

'ir'

bird   girl   first

sir   skirt   shirt

dirt   birthday

'or'

fork   torn   short

born   fort   corn

work   world

'ur'

turn   slurp   curl

fur

The 'a' controlled by the 'w' has the sound as in the words below. Also, we don't really hear the 'w'. So let's review them in these high-frequency words and other common words.

'aw'

saw	draw	jaw
raw	yawn	staw
claw	crawl	law
hawk	paws	thaw
lawn	dawn	

With the 'ew' the 'e' makes the sounds as in the words below. The 'w' is heard.

'ew'

chew	new	news
dew	few	stew
flew	screw	grew

Here in the 'ow' group, the 'o' sounds long and the 'w' is basically silent. But there are nearly an equal amount of words where the 'ow' sounds as though the 'o' is short. The two lists are below.

low	slow	snow
glow	grow	bow
mow	show	row

follow	blow	own
throw	bowl	

The following is a sample of 'ow' words in which the 'o' sounds almost short and the 'w' is pronounced.

now	cow	wow
brow	plow	brown
owl	crown	clown
town	how	gown

shower   down   tower

There are words that end in 'le' and are pronounced as in these words:

tickle	bottle	simple
tumble	jungle	candle
apple	bubble	puzzle
eagle	twinkle	uncle
pickle	middle	wiggle
beetle	turtle	purple

There is a pattern found in words, which is the vowel + consonant + e (or VCe). The 'e' is there on the end to make the vowel say it's name, in other words, for the vowel to be pronounced as a long vowel. The 'e' at the end is silent. This may take some time to master, but it needs to be introduced and practiced.

'a'

ate	same	gave
made	came	case
care	cake	take
lake	base	tape
wake	same	state
plane	game	shape
late	scale	save
safe	trade	

'e'

these   here   theme

'i'

kite	shine	white
like	time	while
wide	drive	rise
side	mile	five
fire	inside	size
fine	describe	ride
wire	mine	

'o'

cone	note	more
globe	slope	store
joke	hope	score
stone	hole	alone
tone	rope	those
bone	nose	

'u'

cute	rule	cube
flute	use	

The 'c' can make the 'k' sound and the 's' sound. When 'c' is followed by an 'e' 'i' or 'y' it makes the 's' sound. When 'c' is followed by any other letter (except 'ch' most of the time sounds like the 'ch' in "chair"), it makes the 'k' sound. This is the rule to follow and learn over time. Use the following chart for study. This rule applies the majority of the time.

When 'c' sounds like 's'	When 'c' sounds like 'k'
ce ci cy	ca ck cl co cq cr cs ct cu

Note: With 'cc' found in words, the first c says 'k', the second may say 'k' or 's' depending on what follows the second 'c'

Practice these words and explain why the 'c' sounds like 's': because the letter 'e' 'i' or 'y' that comes right after it. This may take some time to master. The more practice, the sooner it will happen.

cent	cell	cement
circus	pencil	fancy

In these words the 'c' makes the 'k' sound because the letter that comes right after it is not an 'e' 'i' or 'y').

can	snack	clap
cow	cream	sacs
fact	cut	

Read the following one-syllable, high-frequency words. This list's words follow the main rules that we have covered thus far. Practice these words repeatedly until fluent. Study the list in parts based on your student/child's tolerance.

and	a	weak
in	is	that
it	was	on
as	with	his
I	at	smell
this	from	had

but	not	tools
can	an	each
how	if	will
up	out	then
them	her	him
has	look	see
way	than	first

sit	now	long
down	day	did
get	may	new
sound	year	years
back	things	thing
our	just	good
man	think	say

help	much	right
too	tell	track
want	three	seat
set	end	well
must	big	such
ask	went	men
read	need	land

us	hand	off
play	spell	air
found	still	high
near	add	food
plant	last	keep
tree	light	left
might	seem	next

got	run	feet
night	see	took
book	hear	stop
miss	eat	real
let	cut	soon
list	song	stand
sun	fish	dog

room	sir	steel
red	door	top
ship	black	wind
rock	fast	step
pass	true	map
seen	plan	south
ground	king	town

wood	road	ten
box	wait	strong
verb	front	feel
fact	street	class
rest	stay	green
week	less	stood
ran	round	boat

bring	deep	yes
clear	yet	heat
hot	check	am
noun	six	deal
pair	bill	felt
test	moon	paint

rain	eggs	train
blue	wish	drop
sum	legs	sat
main	kept	job
past	grass	
west	lay	root
meet	soft	shall

cross	speak	son
sleep	jump	hill
bed	free	bright
lead	hair	pound
pounds	milk	lot
act	speed	count
sail	trip	poor

fight	beat	dress
cat	least	gas
foot	ears	glass
skin	brown	cool
cloud	lost	sent
east	mouth	stick
seeds	coast	pay

clean	bit	fell
team	ring	cost
crops	hit	sand
thus	cook	fit
flat	string	thick
spot	bell	fun
loud	thin	rich

send	sight	stream
meat	lift	hat
swim	sell	block
fair	fresh	shop
fear	led	week
win	reach	pass
held		

Let's review these two-syllable words from *Learn to Read Early*, which end in 'er'.

sticker	marker	letter
after	helper	

The following is an additional list of 14 high-frequency words that are two syllables long with 'er' endings. Practice these words repeatedly.

other	number	water
cover	after	mother
under	never	river
letter	farther	better
ever	better	

The following is a list of 5 high-frequency words with an 'a' beginning. Practice these words repeatedly to become familiar with this pattern's presentation and sound.

around   away   along

across   about

The following are two-syllable words following the main patterns we've covered thus far. Practice the list of two syllable words repeatedly at your own pace.

follow   pattern   problem

color   children   products

happen   until   often

second   vowel   hundred

travel   upon   planets

These are 3 syllable high-frequency words to practice.

another   **different**

animal

Try this 4 syllable high frequency word.

America

These are past tense high-frequency words ending in 'ed'. They are two syllable words. Practice them repeatedly at your own pace.

happened   **reached**

covered   **passed**

The **key** to learning to read.

Always, without exception, use your finger to point under the words you read to your children. Do not let your finger skip 1, 2, or 3 words ahead. Keep your finger on that word only, stay under the letter sounds you're on. Don't move your finger to the next line when you haven't finished the word you are on. Be very strict about this. At first it may seem tedious, but this makes the difference between having an early reader and not. With continued practice it becomes natural.

Take the time to learn the letter sounds. On countless occasions I watch parents read to their children, without a finger, and without knowing the letter sounds they teach. For years, parents unknowingly teach their children the letter sounds with added vowels and children take a longer amount of time to learn to read. You must isolate the sound your are making, no matter how awkward it may feel and no matter how you were taught the letter sounds. Please don't spend anymore time not knowing the correct letter sounds, which takes 2-5 minutes to learn. For example /b/ is not "bu", /c/ is not "cu", /d/ is not "du", /f/ is not "fu", /g/ is not "gu", /h/ is not "hu", '/j/ is not "ju", /k/ is not "ku" and so on.

When teaching letter sounds use lowercase letters only, and letter sounds only, don't teach the alphabet at the same time. Make letter sounds even when referring to letters. Think of it as you are making letter sounds the new names of the letters. Children will learn the uppercase letters and the letter names, don't worry about that!

Never rush your child, encourage your child to slow down, always use his/her finger and not to move his/her eyes past the word(s) (s)he is on. Speed reading should not be taught when learning to read.

This is a basic reference chart containing many sounds that have been introduced.

Letters	Consonant digraphs	Vowel digraphs	Silent combinations	r-controlled vowels
a	bl	oo	wh	ar
b	br	ee	igh	er
c	ch	ai		ir
d	ck	ay		or
e	cl	ea		ur
f	cr	ue		
g	dr	oa	'c' with /k/ sound	L-controlled 'a'
h	fl	ey	ce	all
i	fr	oy	ci	
j	gl	oi	cy	
k	gr	aw		w-controlled vowels
l	ng	ow		aw
m		ou		ew
n	pl			ow
o	pr			
p				prefix
q	sk			un
r	sl			
s	sm			
t	sn			

u	sp			
v	st			**suffixes**
w	sw			ing
x	th			ed
y	tr			
z				

About the Author

Cynthia Baugh-Llerenas M.Ed. resides in San Diego California and is originally from Michigan. She has a master's degree from Arizona State University and a bachelor's degree from San Diego State University. Ms. Baugh-Llerenas was invited to participate in research at three neuroscience laboratories in the studies of both cognitive neuroscience and behavioral neuroscience on learning and behavior (both at San Diego State University and the University of California, San Diego).

Contact information:
Email:cindy.llerenas12@gmail.com
Facebook: https://www.facebook.com/cynthia.llerenas.98
Phone: (858) 255-1211

www.ingramcontent.com/pod-product-compliance
Lightning Source LLC
Chambersburg PA
CBHW081349040426
42450CB00015B/3363